Remember Your Death

MEMENTO MORI Journal

By Theresa Aletheia Noble, FSP

Pauline

BOOKS & MEDIA

Boston

ISBN 10: 0-8198-6521-4

ISBN 13: 978-0-8198-6521-2

Cover art and design by Danielle Victoria Lussier, FSP

Published by Pauline Books & Media, 50 Saint Pauls Avenue, Boston, MA 02130-3491

Printed in the U.S.A.

www.pauline.org

Pauline Books & Media is the publishing house of the Daughters of St. Paul, an international congregation of women religious serving the Church with the communications media.

2 3 4 5 6 7 8 9   23 22 21 20 19

Introduction

You are going to die.

The moment you are born you begin dying. You may die in ten years, fifty years, perhaps tomorrow—or even today. But whenever it happens, death awaits every person, whether rich or poor, young or old, believer or nonbeliever. In *City of God*, Saint Augustine described the startling reality of death as "the very violence with which body and soul are wrenched asunder." A terrifying prospect. So, it's no wonder most people try to ignore their impending death or assume it is far in the future. However, ignoring death will not make it go away. And it may even increase anxiety—because the fearsome truth is that death could come suddenly and forcefully for anyone at any time. Only God knows when each person will die so preparation for death is an essential spiritual practice, regardless of age.

Memento mori or "remember your death" is a phrase that has been long associated with the practice of remembering the unpredictable and inevitable end of one's life. The spiritual practice of *memento mori* and the symbols and sayings associated with it were particularly popular in the medieval Church. But the tradition of remembering one's death stretches back to the very beginning of salvation history. After the first sin, God reminds Adam and Eve of their mortality:

"You are dust,
and to dust you shall return" (Gen 3:19).

God's words continue to echo throughout the Hebrew Scriptures, reminding readers of life's brevity, while exhorting them to remember their death. The Book of Sirach urges, "In all you do, remember the end of your life, / and then you will never sin" (7:36). The psalmist prays, "Teach us to count our days / that we may gain a wise heart" (Ps 90:12). In the New Testament, Jesus exhorts his disciples to pick up their crosses daily and to remember their death as they follow him to the Place of the Skull: "If any want to become my followers, let them deny themselves and take up their cross daily and follow me" (Lk 9:23).

Remembering one's death is a practice that philosophers and spiritual teachers, both inside and outside of the Christian tradition, have encouraged for centuries. While the practice certainly can improve the quality of one's earthly life by providing focus and motivation to live well, it could never overcome death itself. Death—

whether the natural death of the body or the death of the soul through sin—has always been humanity's most intimidating enemy and its most impossible adversary. Only the Creator of the Universe—the One who first brought everything into existence and continues to maintain all living beings in existence—could overcome death. In the mystery of the Incarnation, the Son of God humbled himself and took on human flesh in order to defeat death through his own death. Jesus has defeated humanity's greatest foe—permanent death in sin. All that remains for us to endure is bodily death. And Jesus has transformed even this fearsome reality into the doorway to heaven.

The Cross changes everything. With the triumph of the Cross, remembering one's death involves not only remembering one's mortality but also remembering Christ's victory over death: "Where, O death, is your victory? / Where, O death, is your sting?" (1 Cor 15:55). If we belong to the Lord, we need not fear bodily death. Through his passion, death, and resurrection, Jesus has made salvation available to those who choose to enter into Christ's death, be buried with him, and rise with him to new life. Baptism banishes original sin and fills the soul with sanctifying grace—God's own life—that can be renewed and invigorated through the Sacrament of Reconciliation. At Mass, we consume the Eucharist, the Body of Christ. This Body is not the body of a corpse but, rather, the living, risen Body of our Savior who has vanquished death. The Eucharist is heavenly manna and Jesus promised that it would lead us to heaven: "I am the living bread that came down from heaven. Whoever eats of this bread will live forever" (Jn 6:51).

Even if one does not believe the Christian message of salvation, the rich, ancient tradition of remembering death can bring joy, focus, and fruitfulness to anyone's life. However, for the Christian, it is a practice that extends beyond the reality of earthly life and bodily death. In the power of Jesus Christ, the Christian practice of *memento mori* reaches past the horizon of this life and into the eternal happiness of heaven. The Cross amplifies the benefits of *memento mori* because the practice is fueled not merely by personal discipline but by God's abundant, living grace. As Christians, we remember our death in order to remember our Life—Jesus Christ. We remember our death in order that our lives may be filled with the Life of Christ, both now and when we enter into the joy of eternal life.

Remembering one's death is an absolutely essential aspect of the Christian life, not only because it helps us to live well, but also because it helps us to remember what Christ has done for us. Jesus trampled death! *Memento mori* is not a momentary trend but an ancient practice encouraged by Scripture, Jesus, the Church Fathers, and many of the saints. With the grace of God, *memento mori* has the power to change your habits and lead you to holiness. I hope you embrace this ancient and revered practice and make it your own. And always bear in mind—the practice of *memento mori* is more about living than it is about dying.

As you use this journal, you will be in my prayers.

Remember your death,

 Theresa Aletheia Noble, FSP

How to Use This Journal

This journal can be used in a variety of ways besides the most obvious way—as a notebook to jot down your thoughts and reflections. However, if you want to use it in a way that helps you to more consciously meditate on your death, here are a few more ideas:

1. *A companion journal*: This journal can be used along with *Remember Your Death: Memento Mori Lenten Devotional* by Theresa Aletheia Noble, FSP, that includes journaling prompts.

2. *Examen journal*: If you do an Ignatian daily examen, you can use this journal to document your thoughts and prayers. The examen and *memento mori* are compatible spiritual practices, since both involve looking at one's life in the perspective of eternity. (If you don't know about the examen, look it up, it is a great way to incorporate *memento mori* into your daily life.)

3. *Facing fears with trust*: Remembering one's death can cause one to confront some serious and understandable fears. Journaling helps to alleviate anxiety, especially when we bring our worries to prayer as well. One might find that after some time *memento mori* actually ends up relieving some anxiety in your life. However, it is also important to remember that God often gives grace when needed and no sooner, so focusing on our fear is not always helpful.

4. *Memento mori challenge journal*: However you decide to use this journal, try to challenge yourself not only to read the quotes but to also incorporate a *memento mori* reminder to yourself every time you write in it.

A note: Some of the daily thoughts in the journal are unattributed, which means that they were either written by me or contributed by another author.

A good death does not just happen. You must prepare.

_____

_____

_____

_____

_____

_____

_____

_____

_____

_____

_____

_____

_____

_____

_____

_____

_____

_____

_____

_____

_____

_____

_____

*In all you do, remember the end of your life, /
and then you will never sin.*

—SIRACH 7:36

_____

_____

_____

_____

_____

_____

_____

_____

_____

_____

_____

_____

_____

_____

_____

_____

_____

_____

_____

_____

_____

It is folly to be unwilling to think of death, which is certain, and on which eternity depends.

—Saint Alphonsus Liguori

_____

_____

_____

_____

_____

_____

_____

_____

_____

_____

_____

_____

_____

_____

_____

_____

_____

_____

_____

_____

_____

_____

Sorrow not for the dying person; but sorrow for the one who is living in sin!

—SAINT JOHN CHRYSOSTOM

Following God's way leads to life, whereas following idols leads to death.

—POPE FRANCIS

_____

_____

_____

_____

_____

_____

_____

_____

_____

_____

_____

_____

_____

_____

_____

_____

_____

_____

_____

_____

Prepare for death so that you may face it with courage and hope.

_____

_____
_____
_____
_____
_____
_____
_____
_____
_____
_____
_____
_____
_____
_____
_____
_____
_____
_____
_____
_____
_____
_____
_____

Remember your death every day, but also remember that Jesus changes everything.

_____

_____

_____

_____

_____

_____

_____

_____

_____

_____

_____

_____

_____

_____

_____

_____

_____

_____

_____

If we fear not death, we shall entirely escape from death.

—SAINT JOHN CHRYSOSTOM

Keep your death in mind not in order to look at death but to look through death at God.

_____

_____

_____

_____

_____

_____

_____

_____

_____

_____

_____

_____

_____

_____

_____

_____

_____

_____

_____

_____

_____

If you unite your life with Jesus, your death won't be the end.

_____

_____

_____

_____

_____

_____

_____

_____

_____

_____

_____

_____

_____

_____

_____

_____

_____

_____

_____

_____

_____

_____

_____

_____

All humans undergo the suffering of death. Jesus transforms this suffering and makes it a doorway to life.

_____

_____

_____

_____

_____

_____

_____

_____

_____

_____

_____

_____

_____

_____

_____

_____

_____

_____

_____

_____

Serious sin happens when we lose sight of our impending death and life's goal.

_____

_____
_____
_____
_____
_____
_____
_____
_____
_____
_____
_____
_____
_____
_____
_____
_____
_____
_____
_____
_____
_____
_____
_____
_____
_____

Jesus tells us to "Stay awake" (Mk 13:35). Keep your death in mind and avoid the slumber of sin.

_____

_____

_____

_____

_____

_____

_____

_____

_____

_____

_____

_____

_____

_____

_____

_____

_____

_____

_____

Eternal life isn't just something to look forward to in the future. Eternal life is happiness with God who you can begin to know and love now.

_____

_____

_____

_____

_____

_____

_____

_____

_____

_____

_____

_____

_____

_____

_____

_____

_____

_____

_____

_____

_____

_____

_____

_____

Life is a precious, vulnerable, and swiftly passing-away gift.

_____

_____

_____

_____

_____

_____

_____

_____

_____

_____

_____

_____

_____

_____

_____

_____

_____

_____

_____

_____

_____

Jesus saved us from the foe of death because his steadfast love endures forever.

—SEE PSALM 136:24

Consider that death may meet you in the morning; or at evening, that you may sink to rest with the sun. . . .

—SAINT FRANCIS DE SALES

_____

_____

_____

_____

_____

_____

_____

_____

_____

_____

_____

_____

_____

_____

_____

_____

_____

_____

_____

_____

_____

Fascination with death is morbid. Preparing for death is Christian.

_____

_____

_____

_____

_____

_____

_____

_____

_____

_____

_____

_____

_____

_____

_____

_____

_____

_____

_____

_____

_____

_____

_____

_____

Do you not know that all of us who have been baptized into Christ Jesus were baptized into his death? . . . so we too might walk in newness of life.

—ROMANS 6:3, 4

_____

_____

_____

_____

_____

_____

_____

_____

_____

_____

_____

_____

_____

_____

_____

_____

_____

_____

_____

_____

Jesus is the Way to life. Follow in his footsteps and you will find eternal life.

Now, Master, you may let your servant go in peace, according to your word, for my eyes have seen your salvation.
—LUKE 2:29–30

_____

_____

_____

_____

_____

_____

_____

_____

_____

_____

_____

_____

_____

_____

_____

_____

_____

_____

_____

_____

_____

Before each person are life and death, / and whichever one chooses will be given.

—SIRACH 15:17

_____

_____
_____
_____
_____
_____
_____
_____
_____
_____
_____
_____
_____
_____
_____
_____
_____
_____
_____
_____
_____
_____
_____
_____
_____

Lack of virtue makes a person a walking corpse. Choose virtue, choose to follow Jesus, choose life.

_____

_____

_____

_____

_____

_____

_____

_____

_____

_____

_____

_____

_____

_____

_____

_____

_____

_____

_____

_____

_____

_____

Let us rest assured that the remembrance of death, like all other blessings, is a gift of God.

—Saint John Climacus

Our Savior Christ Jesus [has] abolished death and brought life and immortality to light through the gospel.

—2 Timothy 1:10

_____

_____

_____

_____

_____

_____

_____

_____

_____

_____

_____

_____

_____

_____

_____

_____

_____

_____

_____

_____

You lose precious time when you live without remembering your eternal destiny.

You show me the path of life. / In your presence there is full-ness of joy; / in your right hand are pleasures forevermore.

—Psalm 16:11

_____

_____

_____

_____

_____

_____

_____

_____

_____

_____

_____

_____

_____

_____

_____

_____

_____

_____

_____

_____

_____

_____

_____

Fear of death can lead to sin. Jesus offers us the grace to live in his love, without fear of death.

_____

_____

_____

_____

_____

_____

_____

_____

_____

_____

_____

_____

_____

_____

_____

_____

_____

_____

_____

_____

_____

God holds you in existence with his love.

How sweet will be the death of those who have done penance for all their sins so that they will not have any purgatory!

—Saint Teresa of Ávila

_____

_____
_____
_____
_____
_____
_____
_____
_____
_____
_____
_____
_____
_____
_____
_____
_____
_____
_____
_____
_____
_____
_____
_____
_____
_____
_____

A Christian who meditates on death does not gaze on a hopeless abyss but on Christ's victory.

_____

_____

_____

_____

_____

_____

_____

_____

_____

_____

_____

_____

_____

_____

_____

_____

_____

_____

_____

_____

_____

For God so loved the world that he gave his only Son, so that everyone who believes in him may not perish but may have eternal life.

—JOHN 3:16

The Church, the Body of Christ, pours out the grace of salvation on all her children. Do not be deterred from receiving her life-giving grace.

_____

_____

_____

_____

_____

_____

_____

_____

_____

_____

_____

_____

_____

_____

_____

_____

_____

_____

_____

_____

_____

Practice and increase in virtue up to the very moment of death.

—SAINT BONAVENTURE

Some day you will be the guest of honor at your own funeral. Live your life in the way you want to be remembered on that day.

_____

_____

_____

_____

_____

_____

_____

_____

_____

_____

_____

_____

_____

_____

_____

_____

_____

_____

_____

[Christ] has destroyed death. For this reason he came down to earth, that by pursuing death he might kill the rebel that slew us.

—SAINT ALEXANDER OF ALEXANDRIA

Better to die to the world than to lose the indwelling of the Trinity in your soul.

 *Baptism is the entrance into new life.*

The One who has put on the faith of the Cross despises even what is naturally fearful, and for Christ's sake is not afraid of death.

—Saint Athanasius

Kill the sin inside you or it will kill you.

I have set before you life and death. . . . Choose life so that you and your descendants may live, loving the LORD your God, obeying him, and holding fast to him.

—DEUTERONOMY 30:19–20

_____

_____

_____

_____

_____

_____

_____

_____

_____

_____

_____

_____

_____

_____

_____

_____

_____

_____

_____

What would Jesus think of your day so far? That's all that matters.

You are dust, / and to dust you shall return.

—GENESIS 3:19

_____

_____

_____

_____

_____

_____

_____

_____

_____

_____

_____

_____

_____

_____

_____

_____

_____

_____

_____

You turn us back to dust, / and say, "Turn back, you mortals." / For a thousand years in your sight / are like yesterday when it is past. . . .

—Psalm 90:3–4

At least once daily, cast your mind ahead to the moment of death so that you can consider the events of each day in this light.

—Saint Josemaría Escrivá

_____

_____

_____

_____

_____

_____

_____

_____

_____

_____

_____

_____

_____

_____

_____

_____

_____

_____

_____

_____

_____

Baptism is the door to communion with Christ's death and resurrection.

For in that sleep of death what dreams may come, / When we have shuffled off this mortal coil, / Must give us pause.

—WILLIAM SHAKESPEARE

Freedom is found only in Jesus who has smashed the shackles of death.

_____

_____

_____

_____

_____

_____

_____

_____

_____

_____

_____

_____

_____

_____

_____

_____

_____

_____

_____

_____

_____

_____

*Remember the end of your life, and set enmity aside; /
remember corruption and death, and be true to the com-
mandments.*

—SIRACH 28:6

_____

_____

_____

_____

_____

_____

_____

_____

_____

_____

_____

_____

_____

_____

_____

_____

_____

_____

_____

_____

Begin to entrust yourself to Jesus' loving mercy now!

_____

_____

_____

_____

_____

_____

_____

_____

_____

_____

_____

_____

_____

_____

_____

_____

_____

_____

_____

_____

_____

_____

_____

_____

If we live, we live to the Lord, and if we die, we die to the Lord; so then, whether we live or whether we die, we are the Lord's.

—ROMANS 14:8

A good death depends upon a good life.

—Saint Robert Bellarmine

Death, which deprives humanity of all their rights, is unable to do anything against the rights of God.

—SAINT IGNATIUS OF LOYOLA

Evil is real. A battle rages for your soul.
Choose Jesus, choose life.

_____

_____
_____
_____
_____
_____
_____
_____
_____
_____
_____
_____
_____
_____
_____
_____
_____
_____
_____
_____
_____
_____

Christ died and lived again, so that he might be Lord of both the dead and the living.

—Romans 14:9

_____

_____

_____

_____

_____

_____

_____

_____

_____

_____

_____

_____

_____

_____

_____

_____

_____

_____

_____

_____

_____

Live well, and you will not fear death, or if you fear it, it will be with a sweet and tranquil fear: relying on the merits of the passion of Our Lord.

—Saint Francis de Sales

In the path of righteousness there is life, in walking its path there is no death.

—PROVERBS 12:28

_____

_____

_____

_____

_____

_____

_____

_____

_____

_____

_____

_____

_____

_____

_____

_____

_____

_____

_____

Let us prepare ourselves for death; we have not a minute to lose: it will come upon us at the moment when we least expect it. . . .

—Saint John Vianney

Very truly, I tell you, anyone who hears my word and believes him who sent me has eternal life, and does not come under judgment, but has passed from death to life.

—JOHN 5:24

_____

_____

_____

_____

_____

_____

_____

_____

_____

_____

_____

_____

_____

_____

_____

_____

_____

_____

_____

_____

Death is a paradox. Without Jesus, it's an evil, a lack of life. With Jesus, it's a step into life.

_____

_____

_____

_____

_____

_____

_____

_____

_____

_____

_____

_____

_____

_____

_____

_____

_____

_____

_____

_____

_____

_____

_____

Lord, your Cross is the fount of all blessings, the source of all graces, and through it believers receive strength for weakness, glory for shame, life for death.

—Saint Leo the Great

_____

_____

_____

_____

_____

_____

_____

_____

_____

_____

_____

_____

_____

_____

_____

_____

_____

_____

_____

_____

_____

_____

The spirit of God has made me, / and the breath of the Almighty gives me life.

—Job 33:4

Just as bread is the most necessary of all foods, so the thought of death is the most essential of all works.

—SAINT JOHN CLIMACUS

For the atheist, death is annihilation. For the Christian, death is the entryway to life.

_____

_____

_____

_____

_____

_____

_____

_____

_____

_____

_____

_____

_____

_____

_____

_____

_____

_____

_____

_____

_____

The dust returns to the earth as it was, and the breath returns to God who gave it.

—Ecclesiastes 12:7

_____

_____

_____

_____

_____

_____

_____

_____

_____

_____

_____

_____

_____

_____

_____

_____

_____

_____

_____

_____

Jesus turns water into wine, wine into his Blood, bread into his Body, and death into life.

_____

_____
_____
_____
_____
_____
_____
_____
_____
_____
_____
_____
_____
_____
_____
_____
_____
_____
_____
_____
_____

Hail, O light! For in us, buried in darkness, shut up in the shadow of death, light has shone forth from heaven, purer than the sun, sweeter than life here below.

—Saint Clement of Alexandria

Christ died so that by dying he might deliver us from the fear of death.

—Saint Thomas Aquinas

Through the devil's envy death entered the world, / . . . but the souls of the righteous are in the hand of God, / and no torment will ever touch them.

—WISDOM 2:24–3:1

Jesus, when I take my last breath, may you be on my mind and in my heart.

_____

_____

_____

_____

_____

_____

_____

_____

_____

_____

_____

_____

_____

_____

_____

_____

_____

_____

_____

_____

_____

_____

Set me as a seal upon your heart, / as a seal upon your arm;
/ for love is strong as death, / passion fierce as the grave.

—SONG OF SONGS 8:6

Christ's death should free us from the fear of death. Lord, help us to let go of this fear.

_____

_____
_____
_____
_____
_____
_____
_____
_____
_____
_____
_____
_____
_____
_____
_____
_____
_____
_____
_____
_____
_____
_____
_____
_____

The fear of the Lord is a fountain of life, / so that one may avoid the snares of death.

—Proverbs 14:27

_____

_____

_____

_____

_____

_____

_____

_____

_____

_____

_____

_____

_____

_____

_____

_____

_____

_____

_____

_____

If we wish for immortality we must realize that we are but mortal.

—SAINT JEROME

The bed of a good death ought to have for its mattress the love of God [and] two pillows, which are humility and confidence in divine mercy.

—Saint Francis de Sales

_____

_____

_____

_____

_____

_____

_____

_____

_____

_____

_____

_____

_____

_____

_____

_____

_____

_____

_____

_____

Death puts an end absolutely and irrevocably to all our plans and works, and it is inevitable.

—Blessed John Cardinal Henry Newman

Jesus says, "Come and see" (Jn 1:39). We must first choose to follow Jesus before we find life.

Jesus' resurrection . . . illumines the very mystery of the death of each one of us.

—POPE FRANCIS

Keep death before you but have no fear. Jesus has won your salvation.

_____

_____

_____

_____

_____

_____

_____

_____

_____

_____

_____

_____

_____

_____

_____

_____

_____

_____

_____

Of old he threatened our death with the power of [Jesus'] death.

—Saint Leo the Great

Where, O death, is your victory? / Where, O death, is your sting?

—1 Corinthians 15:55

Truly, no ransom avails for one's life, / there is no price one can give to God for it.

—Psalm 49:7

Death as God sees it is not death as we see it.

Live in a way you will not regret on your deathbed.

_____

_____
_____
_____
_____
_____
_____
_____
_____
_____
_____
_____
_____
_____
_____
_____
_____
_____
_____
_____
_____
_____
_____

For if we have been united with him in a death like his, we will certainly be united with him in a resurrection like his.

—ROMANS 6:5

_____

_____

_____

_____

_____

_____

_____

_____

_____

_____

_____

_____

_____

_____

_____

_____

_____

_____

_____

_____

_____

As they pass death by, all who are in Christ trample on it. And, witnessing to Christ, they scoff at death.

—Saint Athanasius

Thus says the Lord God: I am going to open your graves, and bring you up from your graves, O my people.

—EZEKIEL 37:12

All mortals return to dust.

—Job 34:15

Christ is the Way, and this Way is death to our natural selves, in things both of sense and of spirit.

—SAINT JOHN OF THE CROSS

_____

_____

_____

_____

_____

_____

_____

_____

_____

_____

_____

_____

_____

_____

_____

_____

_____

_____

_____

_____

_____

Who can doubt that the Son of God is the River of life, from whom the streams of eternal life flowed forth?

—SAINT AMBROSE

Every day, choose to die in Christ rather than in sin.

_____
_____
_____
_____
_____
_____
_____
_____
_____
_____
_____
_____
_____
_____
_____
_____
_____
_____
_____
_____

Most people avoid thinking about their death. Don't be most people.

To set the mind on the flesh is death, but to set the mind on the Spirit is life and peace.

—ROMANS 8:6

_____

_____

_____

_____

_____

_____

_____

_____

_____

_____

_____

_____

_____

_____

_____

_____

_____

_____

_____

_____

Before God made us he loved us . . . and in this love our life is everlasting.

—JULIAN OF NORWICH

_____

_____

_____

_____

_____

_____

_____

_____

_____

_____

_____

_____

_____

_____

_____

_____

_____

_____

_____

_____

_____

_____

_____

_____

If they come [to kill] me, light the Easter candle and sing Easter songs.

—BLESSED STANLEY ROTHER, MARTYR

Teach us to count our days / that we may gain a wise heart.

—Psalm 90:12

_____

_____

_____

_____

_____

_____

_____

_____

_____

_____

_____

_____

_____

_____

_____

_____

_____

_____

_____

_____

_____

_____

_____

_____

Death is not total destruction but a step into the loving arms of our Savior.

_____

_____

_____

_____

_____

_____

_____

_____

_____

_____

_____

_____

_____

_____

_____

_____

_____

_____

_____

_____

Those who find their life will lose it, and those who lose their life for my sake will find it.

—Matthew 10:39

_____

_____
_____
_____
_____
_____
_____
_____
_____
_____
_____
_____
_____
_____
_____
_____
_____
_____
_____
_____
_____
_____
_____
_____

Your death may come quickly so, every day, say what you want to say to Jesus in that moment.

_____

_____

_____

_____

_____

_____

_____

_____

_____

_____

_____

_____

_____

_____

_____

_____

_____

_____

_____

_____

Living is Christ and dying is gain.

—PHILIPPIANS 1:21

Jesus, thank you for my life.

_____

_____

_____

_____

_____

_____

_____

_____

_____

_____

_____

_____

_____

_____

_____

_____

_____

_____

_____

Life is a long corridor heading toward death. Ignore the end and death may be the end. Look ahead so that you might live.

_____

_____
_____
_____
_____
_____
_____
_____
_____
_____
_____
_____
_____
_____
_____
_____
_____
_____
_____
_____
_____
_____
_____

All is vanity, except to love God and serve God alone.

—Thomas à Kempis

Jesus—not death—is life's goal.

_____

_____
_____
_____
_____
_____
_____
_____
_____
_____
_____
_____
_____
_____
_____
_____
_____
_____
_____
_____
_____

*Now that death and the kingdom of the devil is abolished,
everything is entirely filled with joy and gladness.*

—SAINT ATHANASIUS

_____

_____

_____

_____

_____

_____

_____

_____

_____

_____

_____

_____

_____

_____

_____

_____

_____

_____

_____

_____

_____

_____

Don't postpone holiness. You could die at any time.

_____

_____

_____

_____

_____

_____

_____

_____

_____

_____

_____

_____

_____

_____

_____

_____

_____

_____

_____

_____

_____

_____

_____

He will swallow up death forever.

—Isaiah 25:8

_____

_____

_____

_____

_____

_____

_____

_____

_____

_____

_____

_____

_____

_____

_____

_____

_____

_____

_____

Those who eat my flesh and drink my blood have eternal life, and I will raise them up on the last day.

—JOHN 6:54

_____

_____
_____
_____
_____
_____
_____
_____
_____
_____
_____
_____
_____
_____
_____
_____
_____
_____
_____
_____
_____
_____
_____

In the midst of sadness, remember your death. In the midst of joy, remember your death. In the midst of disappointment, remember your death. In the midst of the celebration, remember your death.

_____

_____

_____

_____

_____

_____

_____

_____

_____

_____

_____

_____

_____

_____

_____

_____

_____

_____

_____

_____

_____

Orient every moment of your life to Jesus, your beautiful end.

_____

_____

_____

_____

_____

_____

_____

_____

_____

_____

_____

_____

_____

_____

_____

_____

_____

_____

_____

_____

_____

_____

_____

_____

_____

Let those who are incredulous about the victory over death receive the faith of Christ . . . and they shall see the weakness of death, and then triumph over it.

—Saint Athanasius

_____

_____

_____

_____

_____

_____

_____

_____

_____

_____

_____

_____

_____

_____

_____

_____

_____

_____

_____

Christ has made death the sweet and beloved friend of the Christian.

God has visited his creature, which he formed after his own image and likeness; and this he has done so that we might not forever be the sport of death.

—SAINT ALEXANDER OF ALEXANDRIA

_____

_____

_____

_____

_____

_____

_____

_____

_____

_____

_____

_____

_____

_____

_____

_____

_____

_____

_____

_____

My desire is to depart and be with Christ, for that is far better.

—Philippians 1:23

In order to live an authentic life, one must face the truth of inevitable death.

All of life is a lavish gift that God gives so that we might do his will.

_____

_____

_____

_____

_____

_____

_____

_____

_____

_____

_____

_____

_____

_____

_____

_____

_____

_____

_____

_____

_____

_____

_____

_____

_____

_____

*I shall overcome death through your resurrection,
O All-Life-giver!*

—Saint Ephrem the Syrian

_____

_____

_____

_____

_____

_____

_____

_____

_____

_____

_____

_____

_____

_____

_____

_____

_____

_____

_____

_____

_____

Let us live so as to die as saints.

_____

_____
_____
_____
_____
_____
_____
_____
_____
_____
_____
_____
_____
_____
_____
_____
_____
_____
_____
_____
_____
_____
_____

Prepare your desire for heaven and let this desire become the king of your desires.

—BLESSED JAMES ALBERIONE

For everything there is a season, and a time for every matter under heaven: a time to be born, and a time to die.

—ECCLESIASTES 3:1–2

Our whole life is nothing but a race toward death, in which no one is allowed to stand still for a even a moment.

—Saint Augustine

All of your time on Earth will be accounted for when you stand before God. Use it wisely!

_____

_____

_____

_____

_____

_____

_____

_____

_____

_____

_____

_____

_____

_____

_____

_____

_____

_____

_____

_____

_____

_____

_____

_____

Listen, I will tell you a mystery! We will not all die, but we will all be changed, in a moment, in the twinkling of an eye, at the last trumpet.

—1 Corinthians 15:51–52

Death is not the time for preparing, but for finding ourselves prepared.

—SAINT ALPHONSUS LIGOURI

Pain and suffering are opportunities to unite oneself to Christ and to prepare for death.

_____

_____

_____

_____

_____

_____

_____

_____

_____

_____

_____

_____

_____

_____

_____

_____

_____

_____

_____

_____

The more you die to yourself the more you begin to live in God.

—Thomas à Kempis

The cleansing fire of God's love in this life allows one to die purified and ready for heaven.

_____

_____

_____

_____

_____

_____

_____

_____

_____

_____

_____

_____

_____

_____

_____

_____

_____

_____

_____

Love and forgive now. Do not wait for another day as death may come at any moment.

_____

_____

_____

_____

_____

_____

_____

_____

_____

_____

_____

_____

_____

_____

_____

_____

_____

_____

_____

_____

_____

_____

_____

_____

Fool! What you sow does not come to life unless it dies.

—1 CORINTHIANS 15:36

This life is not all there is.

_____

_____
_____
_____
_____
_____
_____
_____
_____
_____
_____
_____
_____
_____
_____
_____
_____
_____
_____
_____
_____
_____
_____

Death is not sinister or frightening if Jesus is on the other side.

_____

_____

_____

_____

_____

_____

_____

_____

_____

_____

_____

_____

_____

_____

_____

_____

_____

_____

_____

I want eternity. I was born for greater things than long years.

—Saint Stanislaus Kostka, SJ
(died at age 17)

Thinking about death should lead one to think more about life.

_____

_____

_____

_____

_____

_____

_____

_____

_____

_____

_____

_____

_____

_____

_____

_____

_____

_____

Life is real! Life is earnest! / And the grave is not its goal.

—HENRY WADSWORTH LONGFELLOW

_____

_____

_____

_____

_____

_____

_____

_____

_____

_____

_____

_____

_____

_____

_____

_____

_____

_____

_____

_____

_____

_____

_____

_____

_____

God proves his love for us in that while we still were sinners Christ died for us.

—ROMANS 5:8

_____

_____

_____

_____

_____

_____

_____

_____

_____

_____

_____

_____

_____

_____

_____

_____

_____

_____

_____

_____

God already knows when you are going to die. Ask him to help you to prepare.

_____

_____

_____

_____

_____

_____

_____

_____

_____

_____

_____

_____

_____

_____

_____

_____

_____

_____

_____

_____

_____

_____

Praise our loving God who tore open the heavens and came down to save us from dying in sin!

_____

_____

_____

_____

_____

_____

_____

_____

_____

_____

_____

_____

_____

_____

_____

_____

_____

_____

_____

_____

You are going to die one day.

_____

_____
_____
_____
_____
_____
_____
_____
_____
_____
_____
_____
_____
_____
_____
_____
_____
_____
_____
_____

To die, in fact, is part of life and not only of its end, but, if we pay attention, of every instant.

—POPE BENEDICT XVI

Let us prepare ourselves for a good death, for eternity. Let us not lose our time in lukewarmness, in negligence, in our habitual infidelities.

—SAINT JOHN VIANNEY

Do not wait until the last moment of life to turn away from serious sin. Virtue is its own reward.

_____

_____

_____

_____

_____

_____

_____

_____

_____

_____

_____

_____

_____

_____

_____

_____

_____

_____

Be faithful until death, and I will give you the crown of life.

—Revelation 2:10

Because Jesus trampled death at the Place of the Skull one can gaze at a skull and see life.

There is a battle for your soul, guard it well!

Unless a grain of wheat falls into the earth and dies, it remains just a single grain; but if it dies, it bears much fruit.

—JOHN 12:24

If you thought more often of your death than of having a long life, you would more fervently correct yourself.

—Thomas à Kempis

For a person of faith, death is not a terrifying specter but a path to resurrection.

_____

_____

_____

_____

_____

_____

_____

_____

_____

_____

_____

_____

_____

_____

_____

_____

_____

_____

_____

_____

_____

One day your body will be lowered into the grave and your soul will meet God. Are you living in preparation for this moment?

_____

_____
_____
_____
_____
_____
_____
_____
_____
_____
_____
_____
_____
_____
_____
_____
_____
_____
_____
_____
_____
_____

The Doctor said that Death was but / A scientific fact: / And twice a day the Chaplain called / And left a little tract.

—Oscar Wilde

_____

_____

_____

_____

_____

_____

_____

_____

_____

_____

_____

_____

_____

_____

_____

_____

_____

_____

_____

_____

Be prepared. Jesus may come for you at any time.

_____

_____

_____

_____

_____

_____

_____

_____

_____

_____

_____

_____

_____

_____

_____

_____

_____

_____

_____

_____

_____

_____

_____

_____

You will be hated by all because of my name. But the one who endures to the end will be saved.

—Matthew 10:22

_____

_____

_____

_____

_____

_____

_____

_____

_____

_____

_____

_____

_____

_____

_____

_____

_____

_____

_____

_____

Converse with Jesus. . . . Attach yourself to him with heart and mind, that he may save you from eternal death.

—SAINT IGNATIUS OF LOYOLA

_____

_____

_____

_____

_____

_____

_____

_____

_____

_____

_____

_____

_____

_____

_____

_____

_____

_____

_____

_____

_____

_____

Death is perhaps not far off. I wish to prepare for that great moment.

—SAINT ALPHONSUS LIGOURI

_____

_____

_____

_____

_____

_____

_____

_____

_____

_____

_____

_____

_____

_____

_____

_____

_____

_____

_____

_____

All the delights of this world do not compare to the light and joy of heaven's beatific vision.

_____

_____
_____
_____
_____
_____
_____
_____
_____
_____
_____
_____
_____
_____
_____
_____
_____
_____
_____
_____
_____
_____
_____
_____
_____

For the wages of sin is death, but the free gift of God is eternal life in Christ Jesus our Lord.

—ROMANS 6:23

If you could taste the joys of heaven for even a moment, you would have no fear of death.

_____

_____
_____
_____
_____
_____
_____
_____
_____
_____
_____
_____
_____
_____
_____
_____
_____
_____
_____
_____
_____
_____
_____
_____

When Christ calls a man he bids him come and die.

—DIETRICH BONHOEFFER

When we live for God it is easy to die for God.

By the sign of the Cross, and by faith in Christ, death is trampled.

—SAINT ATHANASIUS

Either we believe in a God of life, or we serve the idols of death.

—Saint Oscar Romero

When we consider how soon death will cut us off, we ought to forget everything, to gain the one thing necessary.

—Saint Elizabeth Ann Seton

_____

_____

_____

_____

_____

_____

_____

_____

_____

_____

_____

_____

_____

_____

_____

_____

_____

_____

_____

_____

_____

Each day you wake up is one day closer to eternity.

_____

_____

_____

_____

_____

_____

_____

_____

_____

_____

_____

_____

_____

_____

_____

_____

_____

_____

_____

_____

_____

_____

_____

Unless we resolve to put up with death and ill-health once and for all, we shall never accomplish anything.

—SAINT TERESA OF ÁVILA

One begins to die as soon as one begins to live.

—Saint Augustine

It is no longer I who live, but it is Christ who lives in me.

—GALATIANS 2:20

_____

_____

_____

_____

_____

_____

_____

_____

_____

_____

_____

_____

_____

_____

_____

_____

_____

_____

_____

_____

As all die in Adam, so all will be made alive in Christ.

—1 Corinthians 15:22

God invites you today to become holy. Don't wait until tomorrow.

_____

_____

_____

_____

_____

_____

_____

_____

_____

_____

_____

_____

_____

_____

_____

_____

_____

_____

_____

_____

_____

How can dust and ashes be proud? / Even in life the human body decays.

—Sirach 10:9

Keep firmly in mind that it is good to always live as though you were about to die.

—THOMAS À KEMPIS

_____

_____

_____

_____

_____

_____

_____

_____

_____

_____

_____

_____

_____

_____

_____

_____

_____

_____

_____

_____

Seek God and you will prepare well for death.

_____

_____
_____
_____
_____
_____
_____
_____
_____
_____
_____
_____
_____
_____
_____
_____
_____
_____
_____
_____
_____
_____
_____

He will wipe every tear from their eyes. / Death will be no more.

—REVELATION 21:4

_____

_____

_____

_____

_____

_____

_____

_____

_____

_____

_____

_____

_____

_____

_____

_____

_____

_____

_____

_____

_____

_____

Every saint in heaven died twice: once to themselves, and once to this life.

Seek good and not evil, / that you may live.

—Amos 5:14

_____

_____

_____

_____

_____

_____

_____

_____

_____

_____

_____

_____

_____

_____

_____

_____

_____

_____

_____

_____

Dying to oneself prepares the soul to receive more deeply the rich graces of Christ's resurrection.

Ask of our Lord a salutary fear of death, and the grace to be ready at any moment.

—Saint Ignatius of Loyola

Every day life speeds toward the grave and, with God's grace, to eternal life. Where is death? Seek it in Christ, for it exists no longer.

—SAINT AUGUSTINE

Cannot the Creator who brought us into existence raise up again that which already exists and has decayed?

—Saint Cyril of Jerusalem

Strive to live your life in the embrace of Jesus' love and you will die this way as well.

_____

_____

_____

_____

_____

_____

_____

_____

_____

_____

_____

_____

_____

_____

_____

_____

_____

_____

_____

_____

_____

_____

[God] marshals the host of the height of heaven; / but all human beings are dust and ashes.

—SIRACH 17:32

Live today with gusto, joy, and soberness, for you never know if it will be your last.

Be ready, for the Son of Man is coming at an unexpected hour.

—Matthew 24:44

Every celebration of the Mass is a reminder of Jesus' death and the resurrection he has won for us.

_____

_____

_____

_____

_____

_____

_____

_____

_____

_____

_____

_____

_____

_____

_____

_____

_____

_____

_____

_____

_____

_____

Is it not in some manner to dishonor the victory of Jesus Christ over death . . . to remain still in slavery through fear of dying?

—Saint Francis de Sales

_____

_____

_____

_____

_____

_____

_____

_____

_____

_____

_____

_____

_____

_____

_____

_____

_____

_____

_____

_____

_____

I am the way, and the truth, and the life. No one comes to the Father except through me.

—John 14:6

_____

_____
_____
_____
_____
_____
_____
_____
_____
_____
_____
_____
_____
_____
_____
_____
_____
_____
_____
_____
_____
_____
_____
_____

Praise God for the gift of eternal life!

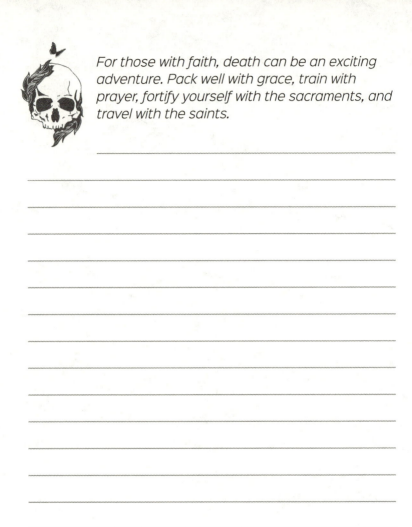

For those with faith, death can be an exciting adventure. Pack well with grace, train with prayer, fortify yourself with the sacraments, and travel with the saints.

When you see someone die, reflect that you also must pass the same way.

—THOMAS À KEMPIS

_____

_____

_____

_____

_____

_____

_____

_____

_____

_____

_____

_____

_____

_____

_____

_____

_____

_____

_____

_____

You were made for so much more than sin.

_____

_____
_____
_____
_____
_____
_____
_____
_____
_____
_____
_____
_____
_____
_____
_____
_____
_____
_____
_____
_____

The Lord is my shepherd, there is nothing I lack. . . . Even though I walk through the valley of the shadow of death / I fear no evil; / for you are with me.

—PSALM 23:1, 4

Do not be afraid; I am the first and the last, and the living one. I was dead, and see, I am alive forever and ever. . . .

—Rev 1:17–18

Fish taken out of the sea die; but the apostles have fished for us and have taken us out of the sea of this world so we could be brought from death to life.

—Saint Jerome

All people are grass. . . / The grass withers, the flower fades; / but the word of our God will stand forever.

—Isaiah 40:6, 8

Nothing is more useful than to frequently and seriously examine our conscience so we may prepare for death.

—SAINT ROBERT BELLARMINE

_____

_____

_____

_____

_____

_____

_____

_____

_____

_____

_____

_____

_____

_____

_____

_____

_____

_____

_____

_____

_____

Rather than build on that which is fleeting—the kingdom of self—build upon that which is eternal—the Kingdom of God.

_____

_____

_____

_____

_____

_____

_____

_____

_____

_____

_____

_____

_____

_____

_____

_____

_____

_____

_____

_____

_____

Make peace with your inevitable death and remember it in all you do.

"Then death will come to fetch you?"—"No, not death, but the Good God."

—Saint Thérèse of Lisieux

_____

_____
_____
_____
_____
_____
_____
_____
_____
_____
_____
_____
_____
_____
_____
_____
_____
_____
_____
_____
_____
_____
_____
_____
_____

The business of the Christian is nothing else than to be ever preparing for death.

—Saint Irenaeus

Without warning, whether we think or think not of it, we shall die; and every hour, every moment brings us nearer to our end.

—Saint Alphonsus Ligouri

[Christ] is God, he is the life and it is he who gives life.

—COUNCIL OF EPHESUS

_____

_____

_____

_____

_____

_____

_____

_____

_____

_____

_____

_____

_____

_____

_____

_____

_____

_____

_____

_____

_____

_____

Death is good to the good, and evil to the evil.

—SAINT AUGUSTINE

Christus is risen from the dead! / Dying, he conquered death; /
To the dead, he has given life.

—Byzantine Liturgy, Troparion of Easter

Ask God to give you a happy death, by the merits of his dearly beloved Son.

—SAINT FRANCIS DE SALES

_____

_____
_____
_____
_____
_____
_____
_____
_____
_____
_____
_____
_____
_____
_____
_____
_____
_____
_____
_____
_____
_____
_____
_____
_____

For here we have no lasting city, but we are looking for the city that is to come.

—HEBREWS 13:14

_____

_____

_____

_____

_____

_____

_____

_____

_____

_____

_____

_____

_____

_____

_____

_____

_____

_____

_____

_____

Let there be in us a daily practice and inclination to dying.

—SAINT AMBROSE

Remember your inevitable death so that you might live a holy life.

With God's grace, try to live the passing moments of life in readiness for eternity.

I am the resurrection and the life. Those who believe in me, even though they die, will live.

—JOHN 11:25

Death follows us close; let us be well prepared for it: for we die but once.

—BROTHER LAWRENCE

Remember your death, choose heaven.

Let us endeavor to prepare well for our death.

—THOMAS À KEMPIS

_____

_____
_____
_____
_____
_____
_____
_____
_____
_____
_____
_____
_____
_____
_____
_____
_____
_____
_____
_____
_____
_____
_____
_____
_____
_____

Think of your death daily and focus on what really matters.

When I find myself on my deathbed, may the last beat of my heart be a loving hymn glorifying your unfathomable mercy.

—Saint Maria Faustina Kowalska

You are a soldier, who stands continually at arms; but a soldier who is afraid of death, will never perform a noble action.

—SAINT JOHN CHRYSOSTOM

_____

_____

_____

_____

_____

_____

_____

_____

_____

_____

_____

_____

_____

_____

_____

_____

_____

_____

_____

_____

_____

_____

Die before you die, so that when you die, there is not much left of you to die.

_____

_____
_____
_____
_____
_____
_____
_____
_____
_____
_____
_____
_____
_____
_____
_____
_____
_____
_____
_____
_____
_____
_____
_____
_____
_____

Death has been brought to naught by Christ.

—Saint Athanasius

Hasten to assure yourself of the sanctity of your death by the sanctity of your life.

—Saint Ignatius of Loyola

The devotion to the memory of the dead is one of the most beautiful expressions of the Catholic spirit.

—POPE JOHN XXIII

_____

_____

_____

_____

_____

_____

_____

_____

_____

_____

_____

_____

_____

_____

_____

_____

_____

_____

I consider that the sufferings of this present time are not worth comparing with the glory about to be revealed to us.

—ROMANS 8:18

Detach your heart from all things which you must leave at death.

_____

_____

_____

_____

_____

_____

_____

_____

_____

_____

_____

_____

_____

_____

_____

_____

_____

_____

_____

_____

_____

_____

If I were on the point of death, what would I wish that I had done on this occasion? I ought to do that now.

—Saint Ignatius of Loyola

Death is daily proved to have lost all his power.

—SAINT ATHANASIUS

_____

_____

_____

_____

_____

_____

_____

_____

_____

_____

_____

_____

_____

_____

_____

_____

_____

_____

_____

It is true, death is hideous; but that life which is beyond the grave, and which the mercy of God will give us, is very desirable.

—Saint Francis de Sales

_____

_____
_____
_____
_____
_____
_____
_____
_____
_____
_____
_____
_____
_____
_____
_____
_____
_____
_____
_____

Let the same mind be in you that was in Christ Jesus, who . . . / humbled himself and became obedient to the point of death— / even death on a cross.

—PHILIPPIANS 2:5–6, 8

_____

_____

_____

_____

_____

_____

_____

_____

_____

_____

_____

_____

_____

_____

_____

_____

_____

_____

_____

We must die! These words are hard, but they are followed by a great happiness: it is in order to be with God that we die.

—SAINT FRANCIS DE SALES

_____

_____

_____

_____

_____

_____

_____

_____

_____

_____

_____

_____

_____

_____

_____

_____

_____

_____

_____

_____

_____

_____

_____

_____

Meditate much on death, that you may not be attached to this life; and on the shortness of time, that it may prepare you for eternity.

—SAINT ELIZABETH ANN SETON

We know life and death by Jesus Christ alone. Apart from Jesus Christ we know not what is our life, nor our death, nor God, nor ourselves.

—Blaise Pascal

All go to one place; all are from the dust, and all turn to dust again.

—Ecclesiastes 3:20

_____

_____

_____

_____

_____

_____

_____

_____

_____

_____

_____

_____

_____

_____

_____

_____

_____

_____

_____

_____

But if we have died with Christ, we believe that we will also live with him.

—Romans 6:8

Draw near to Jesus, he who is Life, to find life. Be healed in mind, body, and soul by his life-giving grace in the sacraments.

Learn to die well and you will live well.

The hour is coming when all who are in their graves will hear his voice and will come out.

—JOHN 5:28–29

Keep death daily before one's eyes.

—RULE OF SAINT BENEDICT

Every day as you wake, give thanks to God for one more day of life.

Live now in such a way that when death comes you can rejoice and not be fearful.

—Thomas à Kempis

Our citizenship is in heaven, and it is from there that we are expecting a Savior, the Lord Jesus Christ.

—PHILIPPIANS 3:20–21

_____

_____

_____

_____

_____

_____

_____

_____

_____

_____

_____

_____

_____

_____

_____

_____

_____

_____

_____

Memento Mori Prayers

These short prayers can be memorized and prayed throughout the day.

Jesus, you did the Father's will every moment, from birth to death. Help me to follow in your footsteps.

Jesus, you want all I do to be united to you, including my death. Help me to begin to prepare now.

Mother Mary, keep me under your mantle and help me to prepare for the day when I will meet your Son.

Jesus, draw me away from the death of sin. Cover me in your life-giving blood and heal my broken, sinful heart.

Jesus, Mighty Conqueror of Death, help me live in you in this life so that at the moment of my death I may be ready to meet you in heaven.

Jesus, Mary, and Joseph, be with me in the hour of my death.

Dear Jesus, have mercy on me in the hour of my death.

Holy Spirit, help me to live a better life by inspiring me to accept the reality of death and filling my heart with Christian hope.

O my Redeemer, grant me the grace to live and die happily in the shadow of the Cross, because you saved me by your holy death on the Cross.

Jesus, help me to grow in trust.

Jesus, I am a weak sinner. Please save me from the death of my sins and pour your life-giving grace into my heart.

Lord, my one desire is to be in a state of grace. Please keep me in a state of grace until I die.

Lord, grant me always to live in preparedness for death. And let me die the death of the just so that I may receive the crown of life.

Jesus, you are my life's goal, my purpose, my everything.

Father, may my life and death be a synopsis of the Gospel.

Sacred Heart of Jesus, as my death approaches, make my heart every day more and more like yours.

Jesus, by the power of your grace, remove the death of sin within me so that I might truly live.

May every moment of my life be a step closer to heaven. And when it's not, have mercy on me, Jesus.

At the moment of death may I say, "Jesus, I trust in you."

Lord, make haste to help me. Lord, make speed to save me.

Lord, save me!

Lord Jesus Christ Son of God, have mercy on me a sinner.

(A centuries-old prayer known as the "Jesus Prayer" that is greatly esteemed in the Eastern churches)

Prayer for a Holy Death

Jesus, Mary, and Joseph, I give you my heart and my soul.

Jesus, Mary, and Joseph, assist me in the hour of my death.

Jesus, Mary, and Joseph, let me die in peace with you.

Hail Mary

Hail Mary, full of grace, the Lord is with you. Blessed are you among women, and blessed is the fruit of your womb, Jesus. Holy Mary, Mother of God, pray for us sinners, now and at the hour of our death. Amen.

Te Deum

An early Christian hymn of praise
dating back to the fourth century

We praise you, O God; we acknowledge you to
 be the Lord.
All the earth worships you, the everlasting
 Father.
To you all the angels, the heavens, and all
 the Powers,
the Cherubim and Seraphim cry out without
 ceasing:
Holy, holy, holy Lord God of hosts!
The majesty of your glory fills the heavens
 and the earth.
The glorious band of apostles,
the great company of prophets,
the white-robed army of martyrs praise you.
Throughout the world the holy Church extols
 you:
the Father, whose glory is without measure,

your true and only Son, worthy of total
    adoration,
and the Holy Spirit, the Paraclete.
You, O Christ, are the King of glory.
You are the eternal Son of the Father.
You did not spurn a virgin's womb to redeem
    mankind.
You overcame death, and opened the kingdom
    of heaven
to all those who believe.
Now you are seated at the right hand of God,
    in the glory of the Father.
We believe that you will come again as our
    judge.
Help your servants, whom you have redeemed
    with your precious blood.
Number them among your saints in everlasting
    glory.
Save your people, O Lord, and bless your
    inheritance.
Govern them, and keep them safe forever.
Through each day we bless you
and praise your name forever; indeed, forever
    and ever.
Grant, O Lord, to keep us without sin this day.
Have mercy on us, O Lord; have mercy on us.
Let your mercy be upon us, O Lord, as we place
    our trust in you.

In your mercy, O Lord, I have trusted; let not my trust be in vain.

V. Let us bless the Father, the Son, and the Holy Spirit.
R. Let us praise and exalt him forever.
V. Blessed are you, O Lord, in the firmament of heaven.
R. Worthy to be praised, glorified, and exalted above all forever.

Let us pray.

O God, your mercy is limitless and the treasury of your goodness is boundless. We give thanks to you for the gifts we have received and look to you for the answer to our every petition. Continue your kindness, forsake us not, and prepare us for the reward to come. Through Christ, our Lord. Amen.

Prayer to Jesus Life

Jesus, Divine Master, we adore you as the only-begotten Son of God, who came on earth to give abundant life to humanity. We thank you because by your death on the Cross, you give us life through Baptism and you nourish us in the Eucharist and in the other sacraments. Live in us, O Jesus, with the outpouring of the Holy Spirit, so that we may love you with our whole mind, strength, and heart, and love our neighbor as ourselves for love of you. Increase charity in us, so that one day we may all be united with you in the eternal happiness of heaven.

Prayer of Praise and Thanksgiving

Lord Jesus, I praise and glorify you for all the blessings you have given me through the abundance of your love, and for the favors and graces you have granted me. You are truly the Life of my soul, the Healer of my spirit, and the Light that guides my path. At the hour of my death be with me so that I might join the saints in heaven to praise you forever. Amen.

Anima Christi

In Latin

Anima Christi, sanctifica me:
Corpus Christi, salva me;
Sanguis Christi, inebria me;
Aqua lateris Christi, lava me:
Passio Christi, conforta me;
O bone Jesu, exaudi me.
Intra tua vulnera, absconde me;
Ne permittas me separari a te;
Ab hoste maligno defende me;
In hora mortis meae voca me;
Et iube me venire ad te;
Ut cum sanctis tuis laudem te.
In saecula saeculorum. Amen.

Soul of Christ, sanctify me.
Body of Christ, save me.
Blood of Christ, cleanse me.
Water from the side of Christ, wash me.
Passion of Christ, strengthen me.
Good Jesus, hear me.
Within your wounds hide me.
Never let me be parted from you.
From the evil one protect me.
In the hour of my death, call me
and bid me come to you,
that with your saints I may praise you
forever and ever. Amen.

Ancient Prayer to the Virgin Mary

We fly to your protection,
O holy Mother of God.
Hear our petitions
in our necessities,
and deliver us from all dangers,
O glorious and blessed Virgin.

Oldest known prayer to the Virgin,
found in a Greek papyrus c. 300

Prayer to Saint Michael the Archangel

Saint Michael the Archangel, defend us in the battle. Be our defense against the wickedness and deceit of the devil. May God rebuke him, we humbly pray. And you, O prince of the heavenly host, by the power of God banish into hell Satan and the other evil spirits who roam through the world seeking the ruin of souls. Amen.

—Pope Leo XIII

Prayer to Saint Joseph
for a Happy Death

Saint Joseph, protector of the dying, I ask you to intercede for all the dying, and invoke your assistance in the hour of my own death. You had a happy passing and a holy life, and in your last hours you had the great consolation of being assisted by Jesus and Mary. Deliver me from sudden death; obtain for me the grace to imitate you in life, to detach my heart from everything worldly, and daily to gather treasures for the moment of my death. Obtain for me the grace to receive the sacraments of the sick, and with Mary, fill my heart with sentiments of faith, hope, love, and sorrow for sins, so that I may breathe forth my soul in peace. Amen.

—Blessed James Alberione

Prayer to the God of Truth

O God of truth, grant me the happiness of heaven so that, according to your promise, my joy may be full. Until then, let my mind dwell on that happiness; my tongue speak of it, my heart long for it, my mouth proclaim it, my soul hunger for it, my flesh thirst for it, and my entire being desire it until I enter through death into the joy of my Lord forever. Amen.

—Saint Augustine

Prayer to Our Mother of Mercy

Virgin full of goodness, Mother of mercy, I entrust to you my body and my soul, my thoughts and my actions, my life and my death. O my Queen, come to my aid and deliver me from the snares of evil. Obtain for me the grace to love my Lord Jesus Christ, your Son, with a true and perfect love, and after him, O Mary, to love you with all my heart and above all things. Amen.

—Saint Thomas Aquinas

Prayer to Jesus,
Fountain of Living Water

Lord Jesus, who was born for us in a stable, lived for us a life of pain and sorrow, and died for us upon a Cross, say for us in the hour of death, "Father, forgive," and to your Mother, "Behold your child." Say to us, "This day you shall be with me in paradise." Dear Savior, leave us not, forsake us not. We thirst for you, Fountain of Living Water. Our days pass quickly; soon all will come to an end for us. Into your hands we commend our spirits, now and forever. Amen.

—Saint Elizabeth Ann Seton

Prayer for a Good Death

Good Lord, give me the grace to spend my life, that when the day of my death shall come, though I feel pain in my body, I may feel comfort in my soul; and with faithful hope of your mercy, in due love toward you and charity toward the world, I may, through your grace, part then into your glory.

—Saint Thomas More

Eternal Rest Prayer for the Deceased

In Latin

Requiem æternam dona eis, Domine. Et lux perpetua luceat eis. Requiescant in pace. Amen.

In English

Eternal rest grant unto them, O Lord, and let perpetual light shine upon them. May they rest in peace. Amen.

Prayer for the Faithful Departed

My Jesus, by your sufferings during your agony in the garden, your scourging and crowning with thorns, your journey to Calvary, your crucifixion and death, have mercy on the souls of the faithful departed, especially on those who have no one to pray for them. Deliver them from their suffering and admit them to your tender embrace in heaven.

Our Father, Hail Mary, Eternal Rest . . .

O God, Creator and Redeemer of all men and women, grant to all departed souls the remission of their sins. With heartfelt prayer I ask that you grant them the pardon for their sins they so greatly desire.

Our Father, Hail Mary, Eternal Rest . . .

May my prayer, Lord, help the souls of the faithful departed, that you may free them from their sins and make them sharers in your redemption.

Our Father, Hail Mary, Eternal Rest . . .

In Paradisum

The last antiphon in the Requiem Mass said for dead.

In Latin

In paradisum deducant te angeli:
in tuo adventu suscipiant te martyres,
et perducant te in civitatem sanctam Ierusalem.

Chorus angelorum te suscipiat,
et cum Lazaro quondam paupere æternam
habeas requiem.

In English

May the angels lead you into paradise.
May the martyrs receive you and lead you into
Jerusalem, the holy city of God.
May the choirs of angels receive you, and with
Lazarus, who once was so poor, may you
find eternal rest.

Prayer for Departed Relatives and Friends

I pray especially for those to whom I owe a debt of gratitude and love: parents, spouse, children, brothers and sisters. I recommend to you especially [*mention the name*] and also those souls who have been forgotten by their friends and family members. Admit them soon into eternal happiness.

—Blessed James Alberione

Prayer for God's Mercy

Merciful Jesus, by your sorrowful passion and by that love which you have for me, I beg you to cancel the punishments which I deserve in this life or in the next because of my many sins. Grant me, Lord, a spirit of penance, purity of conscience, hatred for every deliberate venial sin, and the dispositions necessary to gain indulgences. I resolve to help the holy souls in purgatory with prayers as much as I can. And you, infinite Goodness, infuse into my soul ever greater fervor, so that when my soul is separated from the bonds of my body, it may be admitted into heaven to contemplate you forever.

—Blessed James Alberione

Prayer for the Dying

Merciful Father, with the death of Christ you opened the gateway to eternal life. Look kindly on all those who are close to death, especially [*name*]. United to the passion and death of your Son, and saved by the blood he shed for us, may [*name*] come before you with confidence, through Christ our Lord. Amen.

Acknowledgments

As noted, many of the unattributed thoughts in this journal were inspired by my daily tweets about the *memento mori* skull on my desk (@pursuedbytruth). But some thoughts in the journal are inspired by contributions from some of my generous Twitter friends.

A big thanks to:

@o_crux_ave

@mamascott2017

@YearoutWilliam

@DanielCMattson

@DavidPaternostr

@gardenofalyssum

@SrEmilyBeata

@runner_812

@emersonstevens

@JohnZwicker1

@skytiger3737

@ITGeekCT

@twoboxingfiend

@Brandonbowser45

@CaptPeabody

@pgepps

@FrHarrison

@marybeth_groves

@PontiflexAMDG

@GonnermanJoshua

@CeciliaCicone

@case_adam

@TheAnchoress

@PadreGeoffrey

@FrTimGrumbach

@sisterb24

@florzinha1897

@john_andrikos

@GrumpyinBoston

@PeterPalladian

@jamtoTwit
@JohnZwicker1
@StilleRetraites
@lilligarnett
@FutRelSis
@FatherSJMC
@Kerrygma
@kltherese
@BeatriceFedor
@ianvanheusen
@jmangarteach
@Vallimasoos
@PDeclan
@ConstantCate
@Ivantjr
@erind90
@magnetRN
@BartholomewOPL
@Brandonbowser45
@DocLP
@col_carling
@crisrosie
@YearoutWilliam
@LexieSereda
@EdithofMilan

@Vintage_Sister
@pgk8403
@SanguinElgarFan
@Celeste_CC7
@catholicamanda
@thiscaththing
@sasso333
@2shinewithme
@LuckyEatAnter
@BenedictsCross
@kranco2324
@Lion_IRC
@heatherharper
@CriseldaMortim
@UnapologeticSir
@ggranello
@ajcii
@MyVocation_Love
@Chrisconley7
@DavidApsens
@case_adam
@j_strever
@JRHansen4
@FriarMaximus

BOOKS & MEDIA

The Daughters of St. Paul operate book and media centers at the following addresses. Visit, call, or write the one nearest you today, or find us at www.paulinestore.org.

CALIFORNIA

   3908 Sepulveda Blvd, Culver City, CA 90230   310-397-8676

   3250 Middlefield Road, Menlo Park, CA 94025   650-562-7060

FLORIDA

   145 S.W. 107th Avenue, Miami, FL 33174   305-559-6715

HAWAII

   1143 Bishop Street, Honolulu, HI 96813   808-521-2731

ILLINOIS

   172 North Michigan Avenue, Chicago, IL 60601   312-346-4228

LOUISIANA

   4403 Veterans Memorial Blvd, Metairie, LA 70006   504-887-7631

MASSACHUSETTS

   885 Providence Hwy, Dedham, MA 02026   781-326-5385

MISSOURI

   9804 Watson Road, St. Louis, MO 63126   314-965-3512

NEW YORK

   115 E. 29th Street, New York City, NY 10016   212-754-1110

SOUTH CAROLINA

   243 King Street, Charleston, SC 29401   843-577-0175

TEXAS

   No book center; for parish exhibits or outreach evangelization, contact: 210-569-0500, or SanAntonio@paulinemedia.com, or P.O. Box 761416, San Antonio, TX 78245

VIRGINIA

   1025 King Street, Alexandria, VA 22314   703-549-3806

CANADA

   3022 Dufferin Street, Toronto, ON M6B 3T5   416-781-9131

¡También somos su fuente para libros,
videos y música en español!